AN OCTOROON

BRANDEN JACOBS-JENKINS

NOTE ON BILLING

Anyone receiving permission to produce AN OCTOROON is required to give credit to the Author as sole and exclusive Author of the Play on the title page of all programs distributed in connection with performances of the Play and in all instances in which the title of the Play appears, including printed or digital materials for advertising, publicizing or otherwise exploiting the Play and/or a production thereof. Please see your production license for font size and typeface requirements.

Be advised that there may be additional credits required in all programs and promotional material. Such language will be listed under the "Additional Billing" section of production licenses. It is the licensee's responsibility to ensure any and all required billing is included in the requisite places, per the terms of the license.

SPECIAL NOTE ON SONGS/RECORDINGS

Dramatists Play Service neither holds the rights to nor grants permission to use any songs or recordings mentioned in the Play. Permission for performances of copyrighted songs, arrangements or recordings mentioned in this Play is not included in our license agreement. The permission of the copyright owner(s) must be obtained for any such use. For any songs and/or recordings mentioned in the Play, other songs, arrangements, or recordings may be substituted provided permission from the copyright owner(s) of such songs, arrangements or recordings is obtained; or songs, arrangements or recordings in the public domain may be substituted.

AN OCTOROON was presented by Soho Rep (Sarah Benson, Artistic Director; Cynthia Flowers, Executive Director), in association with John Adrian Selzer, at Soho Rep in New York City, opening on May 4, 2014. It was directed by Sarah Benson; the original music and musical direction were by César Alvarez; the choreography was by David Neumann; the set design was by Mimi Lien; the costume design was by Wade Laboissonniere; the lighting design was by Matt Frey; the sound design was by Matt Tierney; the projections were by Jeff Sugg; the production stage manager was Amanda Spooner. The cast was as follows:

BJJ/GEORGE/M'CLOSKY .... Chris Myers
PLAYWRIGHT/WAHNOTEE/LAFOUCHE .... Danny Wolohan
ASSISTANT/PETE/PAUL .... Ben Horner
ZOE .... Amber Gray
DORA .... Zoë Winters
MINNIE .... Jocelyn Bioh
DIDO .... Marsha Stephanie Blake
GRACE .... Shyko Amos

DRAMATIS PERSONAE

This is the suggested doubling for the play, with actor ethnicities listed in order of preference:

BJJ—played by an African-American actor or a black actor.

GEORGE—played by the same actor playing BJJ.

M'CLOSKY—played by the same actor playing BJJ.

PLAYWRIGHT—played by a white actor or an actor who can pass as white.

WAHNOTEE—played by the same actor playing PLAYWRIGHT.

LAFOUCHE—played by the same actor playing PLAYWRIGHT.

ASSISTANT—played by a Native American actor, a mixed-race actor, a South Asian actor, or one who can pass as Native American.

PETE—played by the same actor playing ASSISTANT.

PAUL—played by the same actor playing ASSISTANT.

ZOE—played by an octoroon actress, a white actress, a quadroon actress, a biracial actress, a multi-racial actress, or an actress of color who can pass as an octoroon.

DORA—played by a white actress or an actress who can pass as white.

MINNIE—played by an African-American actress, a black actress, or an actress of color.

DIDO—played by an African-American actress, a black actress, or an actress of color.

GRACE—played by an African-American actress, a black actress, or an actress of color.

BR'ER RABBIT—played by the actual playwright or another artist involved in production.

RATTS—played by the same actor playing BR'ER RABBIT.

"If such an imitation of human beings, suffering from their fate, be well contrived and executed in all its parts, the spectator is led to feel a particular sympathy with the artificial joys or sorrows of which he is the witness. This condition of his mind is called the theatrical illusion. The craft of the drama is to produce it, and all its concerns conduce to, and depend upon, this attainment."

—Dion Boucicault
The Art of Dramatic Composition

AN OCTOROON

THE ART OF DRAMATIC COMPOSITION:
A PROLOGUE

BJJ enters an empty, unfortunate-looking theatre, mostly—if not completely—naked. He holds a remote control and surveys the audience for a moment, before:

BJJ. Hi, everyone. I'm a "black playwright."

    Beat.

I don't know exactly what that means,
but I'm here to tell you a story:
"Let's find a way to help you deal with your low-grade depression,"
my therapist recently said to me.
"Okay…"
"What makes you happy?"
"I don't know."
"Really? Nothing makes you happy?"
"Not really."
"What about work? Doesn't the theatre make you happy?"
"I mean… Some of it. Not all of it."
"So you're not excited about your work?"
"I mean I'm not-not excited."
"Do you have any career goals?"
"No…"
"Anyone's career you admire? Any professional role models?"
"In the theatre?"
"Yeah—are there any playwrights who you admire?"
" … "
"Anyone?"
"I don't know—"
"Just—just say the first name that comes to mind."

"Dion Boucicault?"

"Who is that?"

"He's a playwright. He's dead. He wrote in the nineteenth century."

"I've never heard of him."

"Yeah—no one cares about him anymore. He's dead."

"...So your role model is someone no one cares about?"

"I mean, people cared about him when he was alive."

"Oh, okay... And what did he write?"

"Um, well, he's probably best known here for
writing this play called *The Octoroon*?"

"*The* 'Octoroon'? What's an 'octoroon'?"

"It's a person who is one-eighth black."

"Ah... And you...like this play?"

"Yes."

"Okay... Well here's an idea:
Why don't you try adapting this '*Octoroon*'—for fun.
I think it's important to re-connect with things
you feel or have felt positive feelings for."

So I did. Or I tried to.

But then all the white guys quit.

And then I couldn't find any more white guys
to play any of the white guy parts,
because they all felt it was too "melodramatic."

I went back to my therapist and she was like,

"Do you think that maybe you're angry at white people?"

"Uh—what?"

"I said, 'Do you think that maybe you're angry at white people?'"

And I was like, "Uh, I don't think / so—"

"Like subconsciously?"

"Um. No. Like most of my best friends are white..."

Then my therapist was like, "Are you sure?"

"Yeah. I am literally surrounded by white people all the time."

"Are you really, really sure though? Like 100% sure?"

I looked at my therapist, who was white.

> *Beat.*

"Well, who needs white guys?" she said, nervously.

"Do you really need them? Why can't you just play the parts?"

"Me?"

"Yes. Isn't 'colorblind casting' a 'thing'?
And isn't that how the theatre started for you? As an actor?
Maybe it's worth going back to the source
of your relationship with this…thing you do."

"Okay…"

"So why don't you try playing the parts you need?
Maybe you'll learn something from it…"

"Like what?"

"I don't know. Whatever it is you learn from the theatre.
Sympathy? Compassion? Maybe even…
understanding?"

> *BJJ presses a button on his remote control and the intro to a
> loud, vulgar, bass-heavy, hypermasculine hip hop track begins
> to play on a loop. BJJ retrieves a vanity table and folding chair
> from somewhere and is starting to set up his makeup station,
> when he remembers something and pauses the music.*

Just kidding. I don't have a therapist.

> *Unpauses it, repauses it.*

I can't afford one.

> *Unpauses it, repauses it.*

You people are my therapy.

> *BJJ unpauses the music again and the actual song plays as he
> finishes setting up his makeup station. He finds a bottle of
> wine or some alcohol in a drawer, opens it, and chugs the
> entire thing. The alcohol has no visible effect on him, now or
> ever. Then BJJ gets into whiteface—possibly tries to cover his
> entire body with it. This should go on for some time. After he is
> satisfied, he slowly turns around and, without taking his eyes
> off the audience, very, very slowly and very, very stoically gives
> himself an incredibly powerful wedgie. He takes the remote and
> turns the music down to underscoring. During the following,
> he continues getting into makeup, touching up, finessing.*

I believe an important part of being a good artist
is recognizing your limits.
So I can respect the pussies who pussy out of a project.

I respect it when they get their "people" to be all like,
"Well, such-and-such doesn't really get the stuff about slaves."
I'm like, "What is there not to get? It's slavery.
And I'm not even asking you to play the slaves.
You're playing the goddamn slave owner."
I mean, God forbid you ask a black guy
to play some football playing illiterate drug-addict
magical negro Iraq vet with PTSD who's
secretly on the DL with HIV but who's
also trying to get out of a generic ghetto with his
pregnant obese girlfriend who has anger management issues
from a history of sexual abuse—
in fact, everyone's been sexually abused—
and someone's mother has a monologue
where she's snotting out of her nose and crying everywhere
because she's been caught smoking crack
and fired from her job as a hotel maid...

>   *Beat.*

(I just made that up... Dibs.)

>   *Beat.*

God forbid any actor of color not jump at the chance
to play an offensive bag of garbage
so far from his own life
but which some idiot critic or marketing intern is going to describe as
a gritty, truthful portrayal of "the Black experience
in America," but the minute you ask a white guy
to play a racist whose racism isn't
"complicated" by some monologue
where he's like
"I don't mean to be racist!
It's just complicated!"
he doesn't return your phone calls?
Then my therapist was like,
"Don't you think you ought to not shit where you eat?"
and I was like,
"Well, what happens if I shit where I starve?"

>   *Playwright enters, also mostly—if not completely—naked and*

10

stands in the back, listening.

"Black playwright."
I can't even wipe my ass
without someone trying to accuse me
of deconstructing the race problem in America.
I even tried writing a play about
talking farm animals once—
just to avoid talking about people—
and this literary manager was like, "Oh my God!
You're totally deconstructing African folktales aren't you?"
I'm like,
"No. I'm just writing about farm animals."
And she's like,
"No, no. You're totally deconstructing African folktales.
That's totally what you're doing."
And I was like, "Bitch!
I'm not fucking deconstructing
any fucking African fucking folktales!
I'm writing a fucking play about
my issues with substance abuse
and then I am attributing the dialogue to a
fucking fox
and a fucking rabbit
to protect identities! *Fuck you!*
Give me a fucking break!"
And, by break, I mean a production.

> *BJJ puts a blonde wig on—the final touch. If the music hasn't
> ended by now, BJJ pauses it.*

So then my therapist asked me about my dreams.
And I told her about this dream I had recently.
A dream I keep having.
Basically, I am being attacked by a swarm of bees.
I am covered in bees. Bees are all over me—
all over my arms and legs, my chest—
all over my neck, all over my face, in my eyes—
and I can't see a thing.
And, I don't know if you know this,

but the majority of deaths resulting from bee swarms
are not from bee stings—
but actually from suffocation.
Basically, bees have evolved,
to locate your breath and they follow it
to your face, where some of them
cover your eyes to blind you
and others climb inside your nostrils and mouth,
causing you to choke to death.
It's all very organized.

       Beat.

But, anyway,
in my dream, it occurs to me that I need to
figure out something to do
before the bees asphyxiate me.
And I start to panic. Every time. And it occurs to me that
I should call for help, and so,
I start screaming. I'm like: "SOMEBODY!
HELP! HELP! HELP! HELP! HELP! HELP! HELP! HELP! HELP!
HELP! HELP! HELP! HELP! HELP! HELP! HELP!"

       Beat.

And then, every time, I realize that I'm screaming.
And that, if I were actually suffocating,
I wouldn't be able to scream.

       Beat.

So I must not be suffocating.

       Beat.

The bees aren't suffocating me.

       Beat.

And, every time, when I reach this exact point
where I realize this,
the bees dissipate. They fly away.
And the point of view changes
to that angle in your dreams
where you sometimes see yourself,
and I could see that

what looked like a swarm of bees attacking me
was actually a swarm of bees
that had come together
for a brief moment
into the shape of a me
being attacked by a swarm of bees
and it dawns on me, sadly, that
I wasn't being attacked by the bees.
I was the bees.
And when they dissipate and fly away,
they leave nothing behind.

> *Beat.*

In other words, I was nothing.

> *Beat.*

So my therapist goes,
"Well, you know, that's interesting because,
you know, the Ancient Greeks believed that
a swarm of bees was actually a sign that Dionysus was present!
You know Dionysus? The Greek god of—"
And I'm like,
"Yes, bitch, thank you! I know who Dionysus is!
I'm a playwright."

> *Beat, into the mirror, to no one in particular.*

"Black playwright."
Fuck you!
You're melodramatic!
PLAYWRIGHT. *(Mocking him, slightly whiny.)* "You're melodramatic."

> *Beat.*

(Off BJJ's glaring, again whiny.) "Fuck you—meh meh meh—breaks—
folktales—actors—wahh wahh wahh wahhh waaaah—bees—
waaaah—playwriting—waaah—"

> BJJ glares at Playwright. Playwright glares back.
> It's uncomfortable.

BJJ. Anyway—
PLAYWRIGHT. *(Still mocking.)* Anyway—

BJJ. *(To Playwright, annoyed.)* Fuck you!

PLAYWRIGHT. Fuck you!

BJJ. No! Fuck you!

PLAYWRIGHT. No! Fuck you!

BJJ. Fuuuuuuuuuck yooooooou!

PLAYWRIGHT. Fuuuuuuuuuck yooooooooou!

The following is in complete unison:

BJJ. Fuck you! Fuck you! Fuck you! Fuck you! Fuck you! Fuck you! Fuck you! Fuck you! Fuck me? Fuck you! Fuck me? Fuck you! Fuck me? Fuck you! Fuck me? Fuck you! Fuck me? Fuck you! Fuck me? Fuck you! Fuck me? Fuck you! Fuck me? Fuck you!

PLAYWRIGHT. Fuck you! Fuck you! Fuck you! Fuck you! Fuck you! Fuck you! Fuck you! Fuck you! Fuck me? Fuck you! Fuck me? Fuck you! Fuck me? Fuck you! Fuck me? Fuck you! Fuck me? Fuck you! Fuck me? Fuck you! Fuck me? Fuck you! Fuck me? Fuck you!

> *BJJ gives up. Beat, before he kicks over his folding chair and exits suddenly, leaving Playwright with the audience.*

Where was I? *(Seeing the audience for the first time.)* Hey, sluts.

> *Throughout his speaking, Playwright very vividly and very intensely picks a mysterious wedgie that's been bothering him. He also seems to become progressively drunker, more belligerent.*

Feck, I'm drunk. How did I get so drunk? *(Re: the folding chair.)* What is this?

> *Looks at it, picks it up, messes with it, seems to recognize it.*

Is this a fecking chair?

> *Remembers something.*

Where is me assistant—me "intern"? WHERE THE FECK IS MY INTERN?

> *Assistant enters, an Indian actor—whatever that means to you—wearing a full Native American headdress and regular clothes. He carries on another vanity table and folding chair. He takes off the headdress and begins setting up makeup and costume for Playwright at one table and the makeup*

14

and costume for Pete/Paul at another.

There you are. Fix this!

Gives him the chair.

What the feck is this filthy motherfecking place?
What happened to the fecking Winter Garden?
You know, I fecking managed the Winter Garden?
Our fecking toilets were nicer than this place.
There's not even a fecking petting zoo here.
Where's your petting zoo, huh?

Notices Assistant look at him.

What? Why'd you look at me like dat?

Assistant whispers something in Playwright's ear.

Wha—? What do you mean it burned down?

Assistant whispers, Playwright collapses.

No! No? No! No! No? No? No! NO! NOOOOOOOOOOOOOO!!!!

Assistant helps Playwright up, who is muttering and inconsolable.

No…No…My precious theatre…no…

Assistant walks the weepy Playwright to one of the vanities, pours him into a chair, and sets up a music-playing device with some speakers. He puts on some old-timey popular music for Playwright. This seems to cheer him up a bit. Assistant goes back to his vanity and starts preparing his own makeup, wigs, and costumes for Pete/Paul. Meanwhile, Playwright clumsily begins to get ready, starting with redface.

Time is like…so fecked up. You know?
Why, you ask? Well, first of all,
I'm apparently not famous anymore,
which sucks. You don't even know who I am.
You got the fecking playwright sitting here—
a fecking world-class famous fecking playwright—
Right in your face.
Dion fecking Boucicault.
You bunch of perverts—Watching me get ready like this.
Can't even get a private fecking dressing room.

There was a time when I ran this town!
I was like the—I was like—
The King of the Theatre.
Everybody hated on me and they were sooo jealous—
Just like they were hating on and being jealous of Jaysus
but nobody could mess with me!
I had the World Theatre at my feet!
Hits everywhere! International hits!
Hits in London.
Hits in America.
Hits in London.
I invented things! I pioneered things!
Like copyrights! Yeah, that's right!
I brought you people copyrights!
And matinees! I invented matinees, bitches!
Look it up!
And everyone loves matinees now don't you? Admit it!
You love matinees!
That's like five things—
Not to mention me many stage tricks!
HOW MANY THINGS DID YOU INVENT?

> *Beat.*

That's what I thought.
I did all that shit for you and what did it get me?

> *Beat.*

Every ten seconds you're reviving
one-a Shakespeare's bullshits.
He was a pedophile—you know that, right?
And a deadbeat dad.
That's right, he was a terrible father!

> *Beat, starts getting ready.*

But, on the other hand,
the nice thing about the future is you can
actually use negroes in your plays now.
That's pretty great. You really save on makeup.
But can you believe you have to pay them?

So we could only afford three negresses,
And my assistant here is playing the other negroes.
I'm supposed to tell you that.
Though he *was* a more convincing negro
than the ones who to came to audition…

>   *Shrugs.*

But that's show business.

>   *Beat, more getting ready.*

'Course, you still can't find any Indian actors—
Hey, where did all the Indians go?
Though, I suppose it's okay.
I was always pretty good at this part…

>   *Beat, more getting ready.*

You know—
my name is actually derived from Dionysus.
You know who that is?
The god of harvest and beekeeping,
wine and theatre—that's who!

>   *Beat, finishes getting ready.*

Isn't that weird?
I always thought that was a little weird.

>   *Beat, surveying the room.*

Perverts.
(To Assistant, re: the music.) I'm sick of this. Change it.

>   *Playwright puts on the headdress—his final touch—as the
>   Assistant changes the song on the music-playing device.
>   Another song starts playing—whatever's super-popular on
>   the radio right now, though preferably loud, vulgar, bass-
>   heavy, hyperfeminine, and upbeat. Playwright perks up
>   upon hearing it.*

(To Assistant.) What is this?
I like this.
Turn it up.
I said, turn it up!

>   *Assistant can't turn it up any louder.*

Then put it in the speakers, you genius!

Assistant finds the remote and turns it up. It makes the entire room quake, which Playwright loves.

Assistant hurries about, clearing the space, and hands Playwright a tomahawk before exiting. Playwright lip-synchs for a little bit before the lip-synching turns into something else. Playwright gets lost in the song. Playwright dances. Playwright headbangs. Playwright fancydances. Playwright stalks his prey before thrashing about with his tomahawk. The thrashing becomes convulsing, the convulsing becomes a shaking, the shaking becomes the music, the music becomes the play. The music ends just as Wahnotee stumbles off, in his full Indian regalia, sloshed and swigging from a bottle, completely unaware of his surroundings.

(I'm just going to say this right now so we can get it over with: I don't know what a real slave sounded like. And neither do you.)

ACT ONE

The plantation Terrebonne, in Louisiana. A branch of the Mississippi is seen winding through the estate. A low-built but extensive planter's dwelling, surrounded with a verandah.

Or not.

(Perhaps it's just a theatre full of cotton.)

Dido and Minnie are discovered. Dido is sweeping laboriously. Minnie is just sort of lying around somewhere, fanning herself.

MINNIE. *(Eventually.)* Do you need help or…?

DIDO. Naw, girl, I got it.

> *Beat, while Dido sweeps.*

MINNIE. You know, if you sweep on a diagonal with lighter, faster strokes, it's a little more efficient.

DIDO. Girl, what are you talking about?

MINNIE. Your arms get less tired and you let the air pressure do the work. Here. Let me show you.

> *Takes the broom and demonstrates.*

See? I learned it from Lucretia over in the hayloft before I got transferred to the house.

DIDO. And your arms feel less tired?

MINNIE. Yes, girl. And it takes the stress off your lower back. Here.

> *Gives the broom back.*

You want a banana?

DIDO. No! Do not get us in trouble!

MINNIE. *(Taking a banana.)* It's just a banana. Relax! Shit, I picked 'em…

> *Beat, eating.*

So what was working with Mammy like?

DIDO. The worst. I'm kind of glad that old witch finally up and died. I already like you much better.

MINNIE. Yeeuh. I ain't never really knowed her, but she used to be taking care of me when I was little and she was mean as hell.

DIDO. Yeah she was.

MINNIE. She be taking care of you when you was little?

DIDO. I ain't growed up here.

MINNIE. You didn't?

DIDO. Naw, girl. I grew up at the Sunnyside place on the other side of the mountain. Mas'r Peyton won me in a poker game like ten years ago.

MINNIE. Ohhhhh. Okay. So you know Chris and Darnell and 'nem?

DIDO. Yeeuh. How you know Chris and Darnell, girl?

MINNIE. Oh, you know, Chris was messin' with Trisha over in the sugar mill for a li'l bit an' I met him and Darnell through her at a slave mixer over by the river before she dumped him because, you know, she couldn't deal with the long-distance.

DIDO. Okay, okay—

MINNIE. Yeeuh. So.

> *Beat, sunbathing.*

Can you believe that Mas'r Peyton's been dead for two months?

DIDO. I know, right? Seem like only yesterday.

MINNIE. You really think Mrs. Peyton's upstairs dying from heartbreak?

DIDO. No. That bitch is dying cuz she's old as hell.

MINNIE. I know, right?

> *Beat.*

You ever had to fuck him?

DIDO. Who?

MINNIE. Mas'r / Peyton.

DIDO. Oh, naw! You?

MINNIE. Naw, he only like lightskinned-ed girls. But Renee, you know, who was fuckin' him all the time, she said he had the biggest dick she ever seen?

DIDO. Really?

MINNIE. Yeeuh. Apparently that old-ass man was hung like a horse.

DIDO. That is gross.

MINNIE. I know, right? And now he dead.

> *Beat.*

Whatchu think of the new mas'r?

DIDO. Mas'r George?

MINNIE. Yeah.

DIDO. He a'ight. He don't seem to really know what he doin' just yet but he'll figure it out. Having slaves can't be that hard.

MINNIE. Would you fuck him?

DIDO. No, Minnie! Damn! Would you?

> *Beat. She would.*

MINNIE. But I kind of get the feeling you don't really get a say in the matter.

> *Beat.*

Damn it's hot!

> *Grace, who is very pregnant, wanders in, carrying something heavy from one place to some other place. The women all look at each other. They clearly don't like each other.*

(*Super-nice, super-fake.*) Hay, Grace!

GRACE. Hi…

> *Grace exits. Minnie watches her leave, then rolls her eyes.*

MINNIE. Ugh, I can't stand her. She is so fake.

DIDO. Right?

> *Minnie goes back to sunbathing. Beat.*

MINNIE. Hey, Dido.

DIDO. Yeah?

MINNIE. You ever thought of running away?

DIDO. Aw, hell naw. What am I going to look like running through this hot-ass swamp? Uh uh.

MINNIE. I know, right? Grace's ass always talking about running away now that Mas'r dead and I'm like, "Bitch, you need to calm your busybody ass down." Haven't she heard these slavecatchers got these new dogs nowadays that can fly and who are trained to fuckin' drag yo' ass out of trees and carry you back? And then, even if you can outsmart these flying dogs, once you free, what you gonna do once you free? You just gonna walk up in somebody house and be like, "Hey. I'm a slave. Help me." That kind of naiveté is how niggas get kilt. I ain't never met a white person in my life who try'na help you escape from slavery. Like, you know? Grace is such a mess.

DIDO. Why Grace always actin' like she too good for everything? And I don't know what people think they running away to. Ain't nothing out there but mo' swamp.

MINNIE. I know, right? Anyway, I'm about to have me another one of these bananas.

> *Minnie goes to help herself to another banana, just as Pete enters.*

PETE. Hey.

DIDO. Hey, Pete.   MINNIE. Hey Pete.

PETE. I see you finished fruit duty already, Minnie. Good job. You settling in all right?

MINNIE. Almost. I like the new servants' quarters but I think my room might be a little haunted—

> *People are heard in the house, coming outside. It's Dora and George. Upon hearing them, Pete transforms into some sort of folk figure. Dora and George enter. Dora looks distraught. George comforts her half-heartedly.*

PETE. *(To Minnie, slapping her hand.)* Hay! Hay! Drop dat banana fo' I murdah you!

MINNIE. *(Dropping the banana.)* Ow! What the hell?

GEORGE. What's the matter, nigger Pete?

PETE. It's dis black trash, new Mas'r George; dey's getting too numerous round and dis property needs clearin'! When I gets time, I'm gonna have to kill some of 'em fo' sure!

GEORGE. But weren't they all born on this estate?

PETE. Dem trashy darkies? Born here? What? On beautiful Terrebonne?! Don't believe it, Mas'r George—dem black tings never was born at all; dey growed up one mornin' frum da roots of a sassafras tree / in the swamp.

DIDO. *(To Minnie, exiting.)* He do this every morning. You'll get used to it.

PETE. *(After Dido.)* Git out, you—Ya, ya!

Minnie and Dora look at each other.

DORA. *(To Minnie.)* Well, don't just stand there. Fan me.

GEORGE. Ha ha ha—How I enjoy the folksy ways of the niggers down here. All the ones I've ever known were either filthy ape-like Africans of Paris or the flashy uppity darkies of New York. Here, though, the negro race is so quaint and vibrant and colorful—much like the landscape. And so full of wisdom and cheer and tall tales. I should write a book. Why, Pete was telling me a wonderful folktale, have you heard it? It's about a rabbit who wants to put on a show for the rest of the animals in the—

DORA. *(Grief-stricken.)* George, I don't understand how you can be appreciating the folksy wisdom of the niggers with your dear aunt in the condition she is in! Why, she's nearly paralyzed with grief.

GEORGE. Yes, yes, Miss Sunnyside. I'm sorry. You're right. It's just that, in the few days since I've arrived from my beloved Paris, my senses have been so overstimulated by all the raw beauty of everything here, the wildness, the very essence of life—I can barely stay focused on the matters before me—

DORA. *(Swept up, flirty.)* Dear George, what poetry you seem to have always at your disposal. When you speak, you sound just like your dear dead uncle—capable of such *(Butchering the French.)* joie de vivre amid this gloom. If you weren't as handsome and finely built as you are, I'd say you were his very ghost—his living ghost. *(To Minnie.)* What are you doing? Stop fanning me!

GEORGE. Well, I must admit my artistic inclinations have probably rewarded me certain sensitivities…

DORA. Ah yes—From what I understand, you were living as an *artiste en Paris? Ouais? (Thinking she's saying something else.) Voo vay voo poo chezamaymwah?*

GEORGE. Uh…well my late uncle did very generously fund my studies

23

abroad in the fine arts. I thought I would make a living as a photographer, but I realize now it was probably no more than a pipe dream—

DORA. Hush. I'm sure that was no time wasted. For I'd love to have my photograph taken with your apparatus.

GEORGE. That could be arranged. You know, I have brought my camera with me. I've been trying to make some improvements on it, you see—I've invented a kind of self-developing liquid which, when applied to the photographic plates—

DORA. Oh boy stuff, boy stuff—George, you are such a breath of fresh air! If only you had arrived here some years before your uncle died—things might have turned out differently! You might have foiled Mr. M'Closky's knavery...

GEORGE. Who is this M'Closky everyone speaks of with such disdain?

DORA. Oh, goodness, you do have much to learn. Thank God you've found me. M'Closky was your uncle's overseer before he died and is the man you have to thank for your family's misfortune.

GEORGE. How so?

DORA. Well, your dear uncle—rest his soul—was bad with his money—but if he thought he knew gambling, that snake M'Closky certainly knew it better, and, by the end of eight years, card game by card game and piece by piece, Jacob M'Closky has craftily found himself proprietor of the richest half of this estate. Now, because of him, you and your poor aunt upstairs have come to the ground.

GEORGE. But the other half is free—

DORA. Yes. And yours, technically, but my daddy, Mr. Sunnyside, thinks that the property is so involved that the strictest finances will scarcely recover it.

> Zoe is heard singing, beautifully.

GEORGE. (Rapt.) Is that Zoe?

DORA. Ugh, yes... (Noticing her runny makeup.) Oh, I've made such a mess of myself. Will you give me a moment?

> Touching up makeup, as Zoe continues singing.

Poor girl doesn't know she's tone deaf...

> Notices George listening in reverie.

Do you like music?… *(Off George's nod, sultry.)* 'Cause I'm a singer, too.

> *Beat, as Zoe finishes her song. Dora is confused and unimpressed by the effect it has had on George.*

I was told that you were seen riding with Zoe around the sugar crop?

GEORGE. Oh, she was showing me the property. What a bright thing she is!

DORA. Yeah, I guess? But she need not keep us waiting for breakfast, though. Pete, tell Miss Zoe that we are waiting.

PETE. Yes, missus. *(Screaming at Minnie.)* Minnie! Why don't you run when you hear, you lazy crittur?

> *Minnie exits with a roll of her eyes.*

(To George.) Dat's de laziest nigger on dis yer property. Don't do nuffin.

> *Pete sits down on a bucket and immediately falls asleep.*

DORA. That Zoe has been so spoiled by your aunt and uncle.

GEORGE. I've noticed all the neighbors treat her with condescension…

DORA. *(Gossipy.)* Don't you know that she is the natural daughter of your uncle, and your aunt just adored anything her husband cared for; and this bastard girl, that another woman woulda hated, she loves as if she'd been her own child…and not a bastard. Zoe has had the education of a lady. I wonder what will become of her when Mrs. Peyton is gone…

> *Beat.*

In any case, George, you should have called on me, darling, if you wanted an escort about the property. I live just over that mountain there. *(Shaking her ring finger in his face.)* I know this place like the back of my pretty lily-white hand. Our families have been historically quite close, you know.

> *Zoe enters, from the house.*

ZOE. Am I late?

DORA. *(Rolling her eyes.)* Yes. Breakfast is waiting.

ZOE. Not if Old Pete is asleep—

> *Kicks Pete.*

Wake up you, silly nigger! Where's breakfast?

> *Pete wakes with a start just as Dido enters with coffee pot,*

dishes, etc., crossing into the dining room. She and Pete make a big show out of attending to George, the new master.

DIDO. Here it be, Missey Zoe. Dere's a dish of hoecakes—jess taste, Mas'r George—and here's fried bananas; jess smell 'em—

PETE. Hole yer tongue! Minnie, whar's de coffee?!

Minnie enters with the coffee.

MINNIE. He'ah, Mas'r Geo—

Pete snatches the coffeepot from Minnie.

PETE. Shut up!

Pours coffee for George.

Dat right! Black as a nigger... You may drink dat, Mas'r George.

George drinks it, loves it.

GEORGE. Mmm!

DIDO. This-a-way, Mas'r George—

GEORGE. *(Offering his arms.)* Ladies?

DORA. Oh, none for me—I never eat. You go on ahead, George. Zoe and I need a word.

Minnie and Dido and Pete and George exit into the dining room. Dora snatches a hoecake off of Dido's plate and eats it over the following.

I find George so sweet. Is he in love with anybody?

ZOE. How can I tell?

DORA. Ask him, I want to know; but don't say I told you to. They say all the women in Paris were in love with him, which I feel I shall be. When he speaks to one he does it so easy, so gentle; it isn't barroom style: love lined with drinks, sighs tinged with tobacco—

A cry is heard off, disturbing her reverie.

What is that?

ZOE. It's Paul and his Indian companion.

DORA. Ugh, why does Mrs. Peyton allow that picaninny to run all over these swamps instead of hoeing cane like a proper slave?

ZOE. The child was a favorite of my father's. Mrs. Peyton couldn't bear to see him put to work.

Enter Paul, being chased by M'Closky, who is trailed by Wahnotee.

M'CLOSKY. See here, you imp! If I catch you and your redskin poaching in my swamps again, I'll cut me a switch and cane the black off of you!

PAUL. You cane me, Mas'r Clostry, but I guess you take a berry long stick to Wahnotee; he make bacon of you.

M'CLOSKY. Make bacon of me—You callin' me a pig?

M'Closky grabs hold of Paul and seizes his whip. Wahnotee grabs M'Closky's arm, forcing him to drop the whip. M'Closky pulls out his knife. It's scary for a second.

ZOE. Oh, sir! Don't, pray, don't!

M'CLOSKY. *(Hearing Zoe, putting away his knife.)* Darn you, redskin, I'll pay you off some day, both of ye!

DORA. That Indian is a nuisance. Why don't he return to his nation out west?

M'CLOSKY. He's too fond of thieving and whiskey.

ZOE. Don't speak ill of poor Wahnotee! He is a gentle creature and remains here because he loves that boy. When Paul was taken down with the fever, the Indian sat outside the hut and neither ate, slept, nor spoke till the child could call him to his bedside. He who can love so well is honest.

DORA. Whatever. *(To Wahnotee.)* Go—back—to—your—people!

WAHNOTEE. *Sleugh?*

PAUL. He don't understand; he speaks a mash-up of Indian, French, and Mexican. *Wahnotee patira na sepau assa wigiran?*

WAHNOTEE. *Weal Omenee.*

PAUL. Says he'll go if I'll go with him. He calls me *Omenee*, the Pigeon, and Miss Zoe is *Ninemoosha*, the Sweetheart.

WAHNOTEE. *(Pointing to Zoe, obviously in love, too.) Ninemoosha.*

PAUL. Where is Mas'r George? We're goin' hunting!

DORA. *(Aside to Zoe.)* Zoe, George can't go; I want him to stay and make love to me—that's what I came for!

ZOE. Paul, Mrs. Peyton is expecting a very important letter. Before

27

you hunt with Mas'r Peyton, you must run over to the landing; the steamer from New Orleans passed up the river last night, and if there's any mail they have thrown it ashore.

PAUL. But I'm afraid to take Wahnotee to the shed! There's rum there!

WAHNOTEE. Rum?!

ZOE. Away with you, Paul. Bring the mailbag here.

PAUL. Come, then, but if I catch you drinkin', oh, laws-a-mussey, I'll gib it you! Now mind.

Paul exits with Wahnotee.

M'CLOSKY. I'm here to see Mrs. Peyton. Where is she?

DORA. Mrs. Peyton is feeling a bit under the weather, but her nephew, Mr. Peyton, is newly arrived from Paris, if you'd like to see him.

M'CLOSKY. This ain't a social call. I bring Mrs. Peyton news; her late husband's banker from New Orleans is dead; the executors are winding up his affairs and have foreclosed on all overdue mortgages, so Terrebonne is for sale. Here's the paper with the advertisement.

M'Closky presents the newspaper.

ZOE. Terrebonne for sale?!

DORA. Terrebonne for sale?! And you, sir, will doubtless try to become its purchaser.

M'CLOSKY. Well, ma'am, I s'pose there's no law agin my bidding for it—

ZOE. Wait! There is hope yet! Mrs. Peyton was just telling me that the house of Mason Brothers in Liverpool failed some twenty years ago in my father's debt. They owed him over 50,000 dollars. She has not found the entry in his accounts, but you two could doubtless help find it. Why, with principal and interest, this debt has been more than doubled in twenty years! Mrs. Peyton received a notice two months ago that the firm has recovered itself and that some funds might be anticipated. I'll go find his secretary.

Zoe exits into the house.

M'CLOSKY. They don't expect to recover any of this old debt in time, do they? It may be years yet before it will be paid off, if ever!

DORA. Well, if there's a chance of it, there's not a planter round here who wouldn't loan the Peytons the money to keep their name and blood amongst us. Now, if you'll excuse me, I must attend to Mr. Peyton, the *new* master of this estate.

Dora exits into the house, haughtily.

M'CLOSKY. Curse these old families—a snooty lot of dried-up aristocracy. Just because my grandfather wasn't some broken-down Virginia émigré or a stingy old Creole, I ain't fit to sit down to the same meat with them. It makes my blood so hot I hear my heart hiss! And the presence of these Peytons keeps alive the accusation against me that I ruined them. If I'm ever to clear my name, I must sweep them from this section of the country. Yet, if this money should come! Bah! There's no chance of it. And if they go, they'll take Zoe—she'll follow them. Damn that girl; she makes me quiver when I think of her.

Zoe enters from the house with the secretary.

ZOE. *(Putting the secretary down.)* Here are the papers and accounts— Where did Dora—?

M'CLOSKY. Stop, Zoe; come here! How would you like to rule the house of the richest planter in Atchapalaga, eh? Or say the word and I'll buy this old place, and you shall be mistress of Terrebonne.

ZOE. Oh, sir, do not speak so to me!

M'CLOSKY. Why not! Look here, these Peytons are broke; leave 'em and jine me; I'm rich and I'll set you up grand, and we'll see these families and their white skins shrivel up with hate; what d'ye say?

ZOE. Let me pass! Oh, pray, let me go!

M'CLOSKY. What, you won't, won't ye? Come, Zoe, don't be a fool; I'd marry you if I could, but you know I can't, so just say what you want. I'll put back these Peytons in Terrebonne, and they shall know you done it; yes, they'll have you to thank for saving them from ruin.

ZOE. Let me pass!

Dora reenters, calling for Zoe.

DORA. Zoe!

Beat, as she senses something wrong.

Zoe, you are needed inside. Mrs. Peyton calls for you.

Zoe exits. Dora gives M'Closky a suspicious once-over before exiting.

M'CLOSKY. Fair or foul, I'll have her!

Opens secretary.

What's here—judgments? Yes, plenty of 'em; bills, accounts with the bank—what's this? "Judgment, 40,000 dollars," surely, that is the mortgage under which this estate is now advertised for sale—

Takes up paper, examines it.

Yes, "Thibodeaux against Peyton, 1838." Hold on!

Takes up another paper, reads:

"The free papers of my daughter Zoe, February 4th, 1841." Why, Peyton, wasn't you smart enough to know that while a judgment stood against you it was a lien on your slaves? Zoe is the child you had with your quadroon slave, and you didn't free her before the judgment! If this is so, she's mine! Though this old Mason Brothers debt—that may cross me—if it only arrive too late—Hold on! This letter the old lady expects—that must be it; let me only head off that letter and Terrebonne will be sold before they can save it. That boy and the Indian have gone down to the landing for the post-bags; they'll idle on the way as usual; my horse will take me across the swamp, and before they can reach the shed, I'll have snatched up them bags—Ha, ha! *(Calls off.)* Pete, you old turkey-buzzard, saddle my mare. If I sink every dollar I'm worth in her purchase, I'll own that octoroon!

> *M'Closky stands with his hand extended towards the house. Music. An attempt at a tableau. He holds the tableau for a while before Dido walks in with a washing bucket and some laundry.*

DIDO. *(Realizing she's walked in on something.)* Oops!

M'CLOSKY. *(Startled.)* Wha-ah-ahh?!

DIDO. *(Also startled.)* Lawd, Mas'r M'Closky, I'se sarry. Woo, lawd.

> *Beat, smiling.*

Is you gonna be out here for a while, or…?

M'CLOSKY. Oh, no. I was just about to leave.

DIDO. Okay…

M'CLOSKY. *(Starting to exit.)* Uh, and would you mind taking this secretary back inside when you get a moment?

DIDO. Yassuh.

> *M'Closky looks at Dido for a second, as if trying to remember something, but gives up—frazzled as he is—and he exits. After a second, Minnie enters, looking for somebody.*

MINNIE. *(Seeing Dido.)* Girl, have you seen Solon today?

DIDO. No, why?

MINNIE. I just rememba'd that nigga owes me four pieces of twine and some pig guts.

DIDO. Girl, you know you ain't never gonna see that twine and them pig guts again, for real.

MINNIE. What you mean?

DIDO. Minnie, you know Solon a trick-ass nigga. Remember what happened to Rebecca.

MINNIE. Wait. Lightskinned Rebecca?

DIDO. Yeah.

MINNIE. What Solon do to her?

DIDO. Well, she had a baby—

MINNIE. She did?

DIDO. Yes, girl. And this one time, Solon was like, "Girl, let me borrow your baby for a second?" And so Rebecca's dumb ass like gave him the baby and then that nigga turnt around and fucking sold the baby.

MINNIE. What?

DIDO. Yes, girl. Apparently Mas'r was about to sell Solon and Grace's baby, but then Solon switched Rebecca's baby out for they baby at the last minute and Mas'r didn't know the difference so he just sold Rebecca's dumb-ass's baby.

MINNIE. Oh my God. That is so messed up.

DIDO. But then Rebecca got sold, too, so.

MINNIE. She did?

DIDO. Yes, girl. Two weeks ago. They tryin'a keep it on the DL, though, because they not tryin'a let folks know they broke.

MINNIE. No wonder I ain't seen her dumb ass around.

>Beat.

(Then suddenly angry.) Uh uh! Ain't no way I'mma let Solon cheat me out of my pig guts like that! *(Shouting.)* Solon!

>*Minnie exits angrily, looking for Solon. M'Closky reenters, stalks over to Dido.*

DIDO. Hi, Mas'r M'Cl—

>*M'Closky strikes her violently.*

M'CLOSKY. And don't you ever fuckin' sneak up on me like that again, you nigger bitch!

>*An actual tableau.*

End of Act One

ACT TWO

The wharf. A camera on a stand. George, Dora, Zoe, and Paul discovered. Dora is posing for George, who is arranging his photographic apparatus. Paul looks on, hidden from the others by his mailbags. At some point, Br'er Rabbit wanders through, unseen.

DORA. *(Aside to Zoe.)* Zoe, the more I see of George Peyton the better I like him; but he is too modest—that is a very unattractive virtue in a man.

ZOE. I'm no judge.

DORA. Of course not, you little fool; no one ever made love to you.

GEORGE. Just turn your face a little this way—It's been a while since I've done a portrait. Look here.

DORA. *(Angling her head.)* Like so?

GEORGE. That's right. Now don't move.

DORA. *(Aside to Zoe.)* I mean, doesn't George know I am an heiress? My fortune would release this estate from debt.

ZOE. Oh!

GEORGE. Okay, I've got four plates ready, in case we miss the first shot. I've prepared them with the instantly self-developing liquid I invented. Now fix yourself. Are you ready?

DORA. Ready!

Dora poses in a completely unsustainable way.

GEORGE. One, two, three.

George takes out his watch. Everyone freezes awkwardly. It's quiet except for a gull or two. Br'er Rabbit wanders in again, pauses, noticing the audience from afar, and wanders back out. Meanwhile, Dora's smile and pose melt into something so hideous it's hard to look at. It goes on for a while and then it's over. George thows down the apron.

Okay, that's enough.

33

PAUL. Why she looked like she was having a tooth pulled?

ZOE. *(Sees Paul.)* What are you doing there, you rascal! Ain't you took them bags to the house yet?

PAUL. I'm gwine! I only come back to find Wahnotee. I lost him! *(To George.)* Say, Mas'r George, take me in dat apparatus? You got four of dem dishes ready.

GEORGE. Get out, you cub! Do as Miss Zoe says.

PAUL. Gosh, wouldn't I like to hab my likeness took!

    Exits, running.

GEORGE. Well, that has come out...clear, ain't it?

    Shows Dora the plate.

DORA. Oh, beautiful! Look, Zoe. Don't you think this will make a lovely gift for a...certain gentleman?

ZOE. *(Looking—it won't.)* Yes...

GEORGE. Will you ladies excuse me for a moment?

    George exits.

DORA. *(Looking at the photograph.)* I like this part—

ZOE. Were you saying something?

DORA. Oh, right! If George would only propose to marry me I would accept him, but he don't know that, and he will go on procrastinating in his slow European way, until it is too late!

ZOE. What's to be done?

DORA. You tell him.

ZOE. What?

DORA. Tease him about his shyness—I'm sure it's plain enough, for he has barely spoken two words to me since breakfast, then joke round the subject, before speaking out.

    Pete enters, puffing.

PETE. Mas'r George! Mas'r George!

DORA. What are you blowing about like a steamboat for?

PETE. You blow, Missus Dora, when I tole you: Dere's a man from Noo Aleens just arriv'd at de house, and he's stuck up two papers on de gates dat say: "For sale—dis yer property,"—an' after he shown some other papers to Ole Missus Peyton, she burst out crying—den I yelled—den de chorus of little niggers, dey set up hollerin'—den de livestock reared up and—den de hull plantation—

Enter George, buttoning up his pants.

GEORGE. Pete, what's the matter?

DORA. You are needed at the house. The sheriff has taken possession of Terrebonne!

ZOE. Pete, did you pass Paul with the letter-bag as you came here?

PETE. No, miss; but dat vagabond nebber take the straight road, he goes by de swamp.

Pete exits.

GEORGE. Come, ladies! I'll escort you back!

DORA. Actually, George, you escort Zoe here. I'll run ahead with Pete since I'm so good at receiving comp'ny. You and Zoe have some business to discuss, uh, regarding the estate. *(To Zoe, aside.)* Now's your time.

Dora exits. George and Zoe are alone.

GEORGE. *(Seeing Zoe.)* Poor child! She must be so sad now, thinking she'll have nowhere to go.

ZOE. *(Glancing at George.)* Poor fellow, he is poised to lose everything.

GEORGE. Zoe, with our ruin, you might be left without a home.

ZOE. Oh, no; think of yourself.

GEORGE. I can think of nothing but the image that remains face to face with me; so beautiful that I dare not express the feelings that have grown up so rapidly in my heart.

ZOE. *(Aside.)* He means Dora.

GEORGE. If I dared to speak!

ZOE. That's just what you must do, and do it at once, or it will be too late.

GEORGE. Has my love been divined?

ZOE. It has been more than suspected.

GEORGE. Zoe, listen to me, then. I shall see this estate pass from me without a sigh, for it possesses no charm for me; the only estate

I value is the heart of one true woman, and the slaves I'd have are her thoughts.

ZOE. *(Truly swept up.)* George, your words take my breath away!

GEORGE. Zoe, your mirror must have told you that you are beautiful. Is your heart free?

ZOE. *(Confused.)* Free? Of course it is—

GEORGE. We have known each other but a few days, but to me those days have been worth all the rest of my life. Zoe, you have suspected the feeling that now commands expression—you have seen that I love you.

ZOE. Me! You love me?

GEORGE. As your husband—under the shelter of your love—I could watch the storms of fortune pass by without a care—

ZOE. My love! *(Realizing, recoiling.)* My love? George, you know not what you say! You? My...husband? Do you know what I am?

GEORGE. I know you are illegitimate, but love knows no prejudice. Has not my dear aunt forgotten it—she who had the most right to remember it?

ZOE. *(Aside.)* Alas! He does not know! And will despise—spurn me when he learns who, what, he has so loved. *(Aloud.)* George, oh, forgive me! Yes, I love you—I did not know it until your words showed me what has been in my heart and now I know how unhappy—how very unhappy I am.

GEORGE. Zoe, what have I said to wound you?

ZOE. Nothing; but you must learn what I thought you already knew. George, you cannot marry me; the laws forbid it!

GEORGE. Forbid it?

ZOE. There is a gulf between us, as wide as your love—as deep as my despair; but, oh, say you will pity me! That you will not throw me from you like a poisonous thing!

GEORGE. Zoe, explain yourself—your language fills me with fear.

ZOE. George, do you see that hand you hold? Look at these fingers; do you see the nails are of a...bluish tinge?

GEORGE. Yes, near the quick there is a faint blue mark.

ZOE. Look in my eyes; is not the same color in the white?

GEORGE. It is their beauty.

ZOE. No! That—that is the dark, fatal mark of Cain. Of the blood that feeds my heart, one drop in eight is black—bright red as the rest may be, that one drop poisons all the rest; those seven bright drops give me love like yours—hope like yours—ambition like yours—passions hung from life like dewdrops on morning flowers; but the one black drop gives me despair, for I'm an unclean thing—I'm an octoroon!

GEORGE. Zoe, this knowledge brings no revolt to my heart. I love you nonetheless. We can leave this country, and go far away where none can know.

ZOE. And your aunt, she who from infancy treated me with such fondness, she who, as you said, has most reason to spurn me, can she forget what I am? Will she gladly see you wedded to the child of her husband's slave? No! She would revolt from it as all but you would!

GEORGE. Zoe, must we immolate our lives on their prejudice?

ZOE. Yes, for I'd rather be black than ungrateful!

> *Beat.*

Ah, George, my race has at least one virtue—it knows how to suffer…

GEORGE. Each word you utter makes my love sink deeper into my heart.

ZOE. And I remained here to induce you to offer that heart to Dora!

GEORGE. If you bid me do so I will obey you—

ZOE. But no, no! If you cannot be mine—Oh, let me not blush when I think of you!

> *Exits, running.*

GEORGE. Dearest Zoe!

> *George exits after her. Beat, before Br'er Rabbit wanders in again, pauses, notices the audience, and seems to inspect it for a bit before exiting. M'Closky enters.*

M'CLOSKY. I arrived just too late, the boy had grabbed those mailbags just as I came up. But he-yo! He's coming this way, fighting with his Injun. The devil keeps him here to tempt me!

M'Closky conceals himself just as Paul enters, wrestling with Wahnotee.

PAUL. It ain't no use now: You got dat bottle of rum hid under your blanket—gib it up now—Yar!

Wrenches it from him.

You nasty, lying Injun! It's no use you pretending to be sober; I ain't gwine to sit up wid you all night and you drunk. Hey, war's e'brybody gone? Dar's de 'paratus! Oh, gosh, if I could take a likeness! Let's have a peep.

Looks at Wahnotee through camera.

Oh, golly, Wahnotee! I see you!

Wahnotee springs back with an expression of alarm.

WAHNOTEE. *No tue Wahnotee!*

PAUL. Ha, ha! It ain't a gun, you ign'ant Injun! It can't hurt you! Stop, here's dem dishes—plates—dat's what he call 'em, all fix: I seen Mas'r George do it—tink I can take likeness—

WAHNOTEE. *No, carabine tue!*

PAUL. I must operate and take my own likeness too—how debbel I do dat? Can't be ober dar an' here too—I ain't twins. Ach! You look, you Wahnotee; you see dis rag heah? Well when I say go, den lift dis rag like dis, see! Den run to dat pine tree up dar and back ag'in, and den pull down de rag so, d'ye see?

WAHNOTEE. *(Reluctant.) Hugh!*

PAUL. Den you hab glass ob rum.

WAHNOTEE. Rum?! Firewater?!

PAUL. Dat wakes him up.

Throws mailbags down, sits on them.

Pret? Now—go.

Wahnotee raises the apron and runs off.

De time he gone just 'bout enough to cook dat dish plate.

Paul sits for his picture. M'Closky appears.

M'CLOSKY. Where are they? Ah, yonder goes the Indian! And yonder is the boy—now is my time! What's he doing; sleepin'?

He advances.

He is sitting on my prize! *(Noticing the tomahawk.)* But the Indian's left his tomahawk! I'll clear that boy off of there—He'll never know what stunned him.

> *M'Closky takes Wahnotee's tomahawk and steals to Paul.*

PAUL. *(Through a frozen smile.)* Is dat the dam Injun creeping dar? I can't move or I'll spile myself.

> *M'Closky strikes Paul on the head. Paul falls dead. During the following, a large pool of blood begins to gather around Paul's head and M'Closky's feet.*

M'CLOSKY. The bags are mine!

> *Opens the mailbags.*

What's here? Sunnyside, Pointdexter, Peyton; here it is—Mason Brothers, sure enough!—

> *Opens letter, reads, motionless.*

"Madam, we are instructed by the firm of…the balance will be paid in full, with interest… You may command immediate use of the whole amount at once if required." This awful letter would have saved all! But now I guess it will arrive too late— *(Hearing Wahnotee approach.)* The Injun! He must not see me.

> *M'Closky exits rapidly as Wahnotee runs on and pulls down the apron of the camera. He sees Paul, lying on the ground, speaks to him, thinks he is shamming sleep. He gesticulates and jabbers, goes to him, moves him with feet, then kneels down to rouse him. To his horror, Wahnotee finds him dead, expresses great grief. His eyes fall upon the camera. He rises with a savage growl, he seizes the tomahawk and smashes camera to pieces, then goes to Paul, expresses grief, sorrow, and fondness. Maybe he starts to make a grave—sobbing and digging with his hands? I don't know. In any case, there's a tableau. Br'er Rabbit may wander through it. Or not.*

End of Act Two

ACT THREE

An interior of the Peyton home. Dido and Minnie are discovered. Pete wanders in and out dropping off chairs, which Dido and Minnie set up. They are silent for a while, before:

MINNIE. Girl, is it just me or has it been really quiet?

DIDO. You know, I was just thinkin' the same thing.

MINNIE. Right?

    Beat, as they work.

Even all these white people are being really quiet. I wonder what's going on today. I couldn't read that sign out front, because I can't read.

DIDO. I can't read it, either. You know it's illegal for us to read.

MINNIE. Yeeuh, but I was hopin' you wuz one of them secret readin' niggas. You know, like Rhonda.

DIDO. Rhonda can read?!

MINNIE. Shh, girl! It's a secret.

    Beat.

They didn't tell you why they got us settin' up all them chairs?

DIDO. Naw, but I'm assuming it must be a party.

MINNIE. Oooh, girl! You know I love a white people party.

    Does a little dance.

Where the likka at, where the likka at—where the likka likka likka likka / likka at—

DIDO. Minnie!

MINNIE. You know they get too drunk to notice!

DIDO. *(A little harsh.)* Can you stop actin' fieldhand for like a minute? You work in the house now! You gotta behave yo'self! *(Off Minnie's reaction.)* I'm only telling you this for your own good. I don't want you to get hurt. You see what happened to Two-fingered Tommy when he got caught stealing from the pantry. Now he only got one finger.

MINNIE. Speaking of, you seen Tommy yet? He was supposed to bring up the milk this morning.

DIDO. No, but I ain't seen Priscilla, neither, with the linens…

MINNIE. Well, I saw Priscilla's drunk ass last night. She probably hungover. She is such a mess.

DIDO. Where you see her?

MINNIE. She came by the servants' quarters last night for a drink and to say goodbye—

DIDO. Say goodbye for what?

MINNIE. I don't know. Maybe she got sold?

DIDO. They don't let you *say goodbye* when you get sold!

MINNIE. Then maybe she takin' a trip? I don't know.

DIDO. A trip to where, Minnie?! Slaves don't take trips!

> *They both realize something's wrong. Beat, before they both exit quickly. Pete wanders in with more chairs, as George and Lafouche enter. Lafouche keeps scratching at his face.*

LAFOUCHE. *(Annoyed.)* I must say that, in my fifteen years of experience as an auctioneer, this is by the far the most poorly organized estate I have ever come across—

GEORGE. Well, respectfully, sir, I've only been here about a week.

> *Beat, watches Lafouche scratch.*

Um. Are you okay?

LAFOUCHE. Hm?

GEORGE. I notice you keep scratching your face.

LAFOUCHE. I hitched a ride here from New Orleans in an uncovered wagon and so I'm sunburned. Leave me alone. What is this one name scratched on the list of slaves here? Number 49, Paul, a quadroon boy? A runaway, I assume? There's been an epidemic.

PETE. Excuse me, sar; but ain't no nigger ebber cut stick on Terrebonne; dat boy's dead, for sure.

LAFOUCHE. Oh, was that the name of that poor little darky who was killed by that redskin? That steamboat captain outside was just telling me he's got a set of deckhands that just loved that child and that if they ever see that Wahnotee fella, they'll lynch his copper carcass on sight.

41

GEORGE. What is Captain Ratts doing here? He's going to invest in swamps?

LAFOUCHE. No; he's here to buy a nigger.

Pete perks up.

GEORGE. Hush.

PETE. Eh! Wass dat?

GEORGE. Mr. Lafouche—maybe Mr. Ratts wants showing around the property. You're familiar enough with the place? Maybe we can convince him to invest in swamps.

LAFOUCHE. Certainly.

Exit Lafouche.

PETE. *(Aside.)* He said "I want a nigger." Laws-a-mussey! What am goin' to cum ob us!!!

GEORGE. Pete! Oh, Pete!

PETE. New Mas'r George, is it true? Are we to be sold?

GEORGE. I'm going to say somethin' to you that has been chokin' me for some time, because there's no one else to tell and I know you'll excuse it because you're a nigger and don't fully understand complicated emotions—but my aunt! She's dying, Pete! She's dying! And she just called me to her side, grabbed at my sleeves and screamed, "Oh, let all go, but save the niggers! I speak not for my own sake, but for the poor people here—these niggers, who have been born here, they will be sold, divided, and taken away! Heaven has denied me children—so all the strings of my heart have grown around and amongst them, like the roots of an old tree." And, Pete, I can't deny this poor old woman her dying wish. I know now what I ought to do. I can't marry Zoe, though I love her, but Miss Dora is in love with me and her fortune would redeem a good part of this estate, so I will sell myself, so that the slaves shall be protected!

Dora is seen, about to enter, but she freezes, overhearing the following, and ducks out with excitement.

If Miss Sunnyside will accept me as I am, Terrebonne shall be saved.

PETE. *(Touched by George's speech.)* No, new Mas'r George! Nooooooo!

Dora is heard singing offstage, the same song Zoe sang in the first act, but horribly. She enters from upstairs.

GEORGE. Go, Pete! Go! You must go and tell the others!

Pete exits.

DORA. Poor Mrs. Peyton.

GEORGE. Miss Sunnyside—

DORA. Yes?

GEORGE. Uh, permit me to speak?

DORA. Oh, dear.

Enter Zoe, who stops before she is seen.

GEORGE. *(Awkwardly, reluctantly.)* In a word, I have seen and admired you! And, if you would pardon the abruptness of the question, do you think the sincere devotion of my life to yours would succeed?

DORA. *(Aside.)* He has the strangest way of making love. European I suppose…

GEORGE. You are silent?

DORA. Mr. Peyton, I presume you have hesitated to make this avowal because you feared, in the present condition of affairs here, your object might be misconstrued, and that your attention was rather to my fortune than to myself.

Beat, no reponse.

I mean, you feared I might not give you credit for sincere and pure feelings. Well, you wrong me. I don't think you capable of anything else—

GEORGE. No, I hesitated because an attachment I had formed before I had the pleasure of seeing you had not altogether died out.

Beat.

DORA. One of those sirens of Paris, I presume. I shall endeavor not to be jealous of the past. But now that vagrant love is—faded?— Is it not?

GEORGE. Miss Sunnyside, I have not learned to lie.

DORA. Good gracious—who wants you to?

GEORGE. I do, but I can't. No, the love I speak of is not what you suppose—It is a passion that has grown up here since I arrived; but it is hopeless and must perish.

DORA. Here?! Since you arrived? Impossible: you have seen no one; whom can you mean?

ZOE. *(Advancing.)* Me.

GEORGE. Zoe!

DORA. You?

ZOE. Forgive him, Dora. You are right. He is incapable of any but sincere and pure feelings. You know you can't be jealous of a poor creature like me. He loves me—but what of that? If he caught the fever, were stung by a snake, or possessed of any other poisonous or unclean thing, you could pity, tend, and love him through it, and for your gentle care he would love you in return. Well, is he not thus afflicted now? He loves an octoroon.

GEORGE. Zoe, you break my heart!

DORA. At college they said I was a fool. Pretty—very pretty!—but a fool. I'm afraid they must be right; am I missing something here? I don't get a word of all this.

ZOE. Dear Dora, try to understand it with your heart. You love George; I know it; and you deserve to be loved by him. And he will—he must. His love for me shall pass away. You heard him say it was hopeless. Oh, forgive him and me!

DORA. *(Weeping.)* Oh, why did he speak to me at all then? You've made me cry and I hate you both!

> *Dora exits just as Lafouche enters.*

LAFOUCHE. I'm sorry to intrude, but the business I came upon will excuse me.

ZOE. Perhaps I had better go.

LAFOUCHE. Well, as it concerns you, perhaps you better stay.

GEORGE. Concerns Zoe?

LAFOUCHE. The list of your slaves is incomplete, sir—It wants one.

GEORGE. The boy Paul—we know it.

LAFOUCHE. No, sir, you have omitted the octoroon girl, Zoe.

GEORGE. Zoe?!

ZOE. Me?!

LAFOUCHE. *(Showing papers to Zoe.)* Pardon me, ma'am, but do you know these papers?

ZOE. Yes, they are my free papers; but they were in my father's secretary. How came they in your possession?

LAFOUCHE. Mr. M'Closky found them.

ZOE. Found them? He purloined them!

LAFOUCHE. At the time Mr. Peyton executed those free papers to his infant slave, a judgment stood recorded against him; while that was on record he had no right to do away with his property. That judgment still exists. Under it and others this estate is sold today. Those free papers aren't worth the ink that's on 'em.

GEORGE. Zoe a slave! It is impossible! My uncle was negligent and doubtless forgot this small formality. But surely the creditors will not claim the gal?

LAFOUCHE. One of the principal mortgagees has made the demand.

ZOE. M'Closky!

GEORGE. It cannot be! It shall not be!

LAFOUCHE. It must be. The proceeds of this sale must cover the debts of the estate. Excuse me.

Lafouche exits.

GEORGE. Damn those Mason Brothers, why couldn't they send something by the last mail? Even a letter, promising something! Zoe, they shall not take you from us while I live!

ZOE. Don't be a fool; M'Closky would kill you, and then take me, just as soon as—

GEORGE. Stop—Dora Sunnyside! She'll buy you; that'll save you, if not the estate.

ZOE. Not after we've confessed to her that we love each other—

GEORGE. Right! Why did we do that?!

ZOE. Because it was the truth, and I had rather be a slave with a free soul than remain free with a slavish, deceitful heart.

GEORGE. Zoe!

ZOE. Do not weep, dear George. Be a man. You now see what a miserable thing I am. Leave me now. I would be alone a little while.

George exits, weeping.

A slave! A slave! Is this a dream—for my brain reels with the blow? Sold! And M'Closky, my master—oh!

Falls on her knees, face in her hands.

No—no master but one. George—George—So like my father! My dear, dear father! Have I slept upon the benefits I received, and never saw, never felt, never knew that I was ungrateful? Let me be sold then, that I may free your name and give you back the liberty you bestowed upon me; for I can never repay the love you bore your poor octoroon child. Forgive her. You made her life too happy, and now these tears will flow. Let me bide them till I teach my heart. Oh, my—my heart!—Hush—they come for me! Save me! No—

Looks off towards a commotion.

'Tis Pete and the servants—they come this way.

Zoe exits with a low, wailing, suffocating cry, just as Pete, Minnie, Dido, and pregnant Grace enter.

PETE. Cum yer now! Stand round! I've got to talk to you house darkies—Grace, you might as well hear dis, too.

MINNIE. Pete—!

PETE. Don't make no noise, de sick missus har us! My colored ladies, dar's mighty bad news gone round—

MINNIE. Pete—

PETE. Shut up! Dis yer prop'ty to be sold—old Terrebonne—whar we all been raised—dey's gwine to take it away—

DIDO. But Pete—

PETE. Hold quiet, you trash o' niggers! And dis ain't all. Now listen— we tought dat de niggers would always belong to de ole missus, and if she lost Terrebonne, we must live dere and simply hire ourselves out so we could bring our wages to her—

MINNIE. Seriously, Pete…

PETE. Hush! But I tell ye, 'tain't so—we've got to be sold—

DIDO. *(To Minnie.)* That's what's going on.

PETE. Will you hush?! Now, I listen dar jess now to Mas'r George—You shoulda seen dem big tears in his eyes. He say de missus say, "'Tain't for de land I keer, but for dem poor niggers—dey'll be sold." "But no," says

46

he. "I'd rather sell myself fust; de niggers, dey shan't suffer." *(Getting emotional.)* Yes, for you, for me, dem white folks cried. Dey cried! Fo' us! Fo' us sorry, no good nothing niggers. Now, I say, as dat ole man was always so good to us and dat ole woman—for de pride of de family, let every darky do his best for dey sake—so dem strangers from Nawleens shall say, "Dem's happy darkies, dem's a fine set of niggers!" and they'll buy us right up! And everyone say, when he's sold, "Lor' bless dis yer family I'm gwine out of, and pray send me to as good a home!"

> *Beat. The women all look at each other. Minnie tries to start a slow clap.*

GRACE. What the hell is wrong witchu?! Don't you know everybody done run away?!

PETE. WHAT?!

DIDO. That's what we been tryin'a tell yo' black ass for the last ten minutes.

PETE. What you mean they done run away? Why didn't somebody tell me?

MINNIE. Ain't nobody told us, neither, nigga! Obviously.

PETE. But Grace—you still here—I thought you wuz head of the Runaway Plannin' Committee with Solon.

GRACE. I was.

PETE. Well, what happened?

GRACE. I overslept, nigga. Shit. Mind yo' own business.

PETE. Aw, dis is da worst! Dis is da worst! *(To Grace.)* How did this happen?

GRACE. Eber since sweet little Paul was kilt, folks figguh'd things was taking a turn for da worse, so Solon thought it was time to take off while all these white people wuz distracted with they personal financial drama.

PETE. Laws-a-mussey! Get out of my way! I need to go tell a white man what's going on!

> *Pete exits, running. Beat, during which the women look at each other.*

MINNIE. Well, at least this explains what all them people was doing walking around.

DIDO. You overslept?

GRACE. Yes, bitch. I'm pregnant. I'm allowed to oversleep sometimes. Shit.

DIDO. Okay, where did the attitude just come from?

MINNIE. Solon couldn't wake you up?

> *Beat. Grace starts crying softly. Minnie goes to comfort her.*

Oh, girl, what's wrong?

GRACE. I think Solon left me.

MINNIE. Whaaaaat?

GRACE. I think he ran off wit dumb-ass Rebecca!

MINNIE. Lightskinned Rebecca?

GRACE. Yes.

DIDO. I thought Rebecca got sold.

GRACE. No. Rebecca baby got sold.

DIDO. No, I thought Rebecca got sold last week to the Duponts.

GRACE. No, girl, that was Lucretia from the hayloft.

MINNIE. Lucretia got sold?!

GRACE. Yes.

MINNIE. Damn. There are too many niggas coming and going on
around here—I can barely keep track.

GRACE. Ain't no need to keep track no mo'...

MINNIE. Why not?

DIDO. Because everybody except us ran away, stupid!

MINNIE. Oh, yeah.

GRACE. And now we're about to get sold!

MINNIE. Oh, yeah!

DIDO. This is about the worst damn day of my life! It's even worse
than the first time I got sold!

MINNIE. Yeah, I didn't wake up thinkin' this was where my day was
gonna go. I can't believe nobody told us they was running away. Why
didn't they tell us, Grace?

DIDO. Yeah. You would know.

GRACE. You house niggas.

DIDO. What?

GRACE. You house niggas. Y'all was livin it up in the damn house all the time, serving everybody pancakes and shit while we wuz in the fields all day hoeing cane and picking a fuckton of cotton in this hot-ass sun, so we figured y'all probably didn't need to run away.

DIDO. Well you still coulda asked us. That would have been the polite thing to do 'steada acting like a bunch of selfish fieldhands.

GRACE. And nobody likes y'all!

DIDO. Excuse me?

GRACE. There, I said it. Everyone thinks you're a bitch, Dido. And everyone finds the way you act kinda ghetto, Minnie. It's embarrassing to the community.

MINNIE. What?! WHO GHETTO?!

Minnie rushes at Grace. Grace rushes at Minnie.

DIDO. *(Breaking it up.)* Hey! Hey! HEY!

MINNIE. She lucky she pregnant!

DIDO. There no use fighting about it now!

The women cool off.

GRACE. You right. You right.

DIDO. So Solon took y'all baby, too?

GRACE. What are you talking about? The baby is in my belly?

MINNIE. No, girl, your other baby!

GRACE. *(Genuinely upset.)* Oh, shit, where is my other baby!

Grace exits, running.

MINNIE. Girl, what are we gonna do?

DIDO. I don't know. I kind of liked it here.

MINNIE. Me too. I feel bad for da Peytons.

DIDO. Why?

MINNIE. I don't know. They were some cool-ass white people. I mean, they didn't never *really* beat us, you know? It coulda been worse.

DIDO. Yeah. I heard on the M'Closky plantation they actually, like, whips the slaves. With, like, a whip.

49

MINNIE. Whaaat?

DIDO. I know, right?

MINNIE. I am not tryin'a get bought by Mas'r M'Closky!

DIDO. Well, I saw him in that group of white men walking around inspecting things.

MINNIE. Oh no! *(Remembers something, whispering.)* Wait, girl! You know who else I saw in that group?

DIDO. Who?

MINNIE. That fine-ass white man who own that steamboat. With the tan? I think his name is like Rat or sum'n. Ratts? Ratty? Rabbit? Ratface? I don't know. We gotta get bought by him, girl! Imagine if we lived on a steamboat, coasting up and down the river, lookin' fly, wind whipping at our hair and our slave tunics and shit, and we surrounded by all these fine, muscle-y boat niggas who ain't been wit a woman in years?

DIDO. I don't know, Minnie, that sounds kinda dangerous…

MINNIE. Girl come on. You yourself said you was tired of being in this damn swamp all the time. And I been on this plantation my entire life. I'm tired of all this dirt and dust and nasty-ass table scrap food. Girl, don't you know on a boat they be eating fresh fish and skrimps and stuff? None of these fattening pig guts. Come on, girl, this is our chance to see the world!

DIDO. See the world? What world?

MINNIE. Girl, come on! I gotta idea!

> *Dido and Minnie exit and, after a beat, Ratts, the steamboat captain, enters from the audience, looking for special seating, on account of his obesity. Perhaps he picks a fight with an audience member, whom he accuses of sitting in his seat. At some point, Lafouche has to enter and direct Ratts towards the row of seats Dido and Minnie have just set up. George and M'Closky, both played by BJJ, enter and join him. Time has passed and we are now at the auction. There is either 1 or 99 people playing various bidders. Or maybe there's some clever way to force the audience into doing this. Really all we need is one person to play Captain Ratts. But I guess I worry about the*

whole thing becoming too Brechtian? Though, does it matter? Also, can I help it? Or maybe it's just whoever's been playing music this whole time? Or maybe it's just me? Maybe I sit in the audience of every show and play Ratts. Or maybe it's Br'er Rabbit? Let's just say it's Br'er Rabbit.

LAFOUCHE. Well, I guess this is everyone that's going to show up. Captain Ratts, there's a seat down here in the front row. Don't be shy.

Ratts takes his seat.

Thank you, Captain. *(Fast auction-speak.)* Gentlemen, we shall proceed to business. It ain't necessary for me to dilate, describe, or enumerate; Terrebonne is known to you as one of the richest bits of sile in Louisiana. So, gentlemen, as life is short, we'll start right off. Now, I'm proud to submit to you the finest lot of fieldhands and house servants that was ever offered. Send in the niggers!

Pete, Grace, Minnie, and Dido all shuffle in awkwardly. Pete is grinning a lot and wearing shackles for no real reason. Minnie and Dido are wearing remarkably sexier and more revealing slave tunics and have their hair and makeup done up accordingly. They spot Ratts and make a lot of suggestive faces and gestures in his direction. Lafouche is confused.

Where are the rest of the niggers?

Pete and George share a look before George, embarrassed, rushes up to whisper something into Lafouche's ear.

What?! What do you mean they've all run away?

RATTS. What?!

PETE. *(Clearing his throat, gesturing to the four of them.)* Ah-ah-ahem. Hello?

RATTS. Now wait a minute—Why did you all remain?

MINNIE. Nobody told us.

Lafouche bangs the gavel.

LAFOUCHE. Listen, we're going to proceed because I've got two more auctions today and I have to be back to New Orleans by five, so let's start with... *(Going through his notes.)* Number... *(Giving up.)* Pete, a house servant.

PETE. Dat's me—yer, I'm comin'—stand around dar.

51

Pete tumbles upon the table.

LAFOUCHE. Aged…seventy…two?

PETE. Fo'ty-six, sar.

LAFOUCHE. And lame.

PETE. But dat don't mean nuthin'! Look ye here!

> *Pete starts to sing a very unimpressive, folksier version of whatever song Zoe and Dora sang earlier, before he gives up.*

You know what? I'm tired of being a slave.

LAFOUCHE. What?!

PETE. Psych! *(Addressing the crowd.)* What do you say gentlemen? Shall we start the bidding at a million?

LAFOUCHE. *(Annoyed, stopping him.)* One hundred dollars! Do I hear one hundred dollars?

GEORGE. One hundred.

PETE. Mas'r George—ah, no, sar—don't buy me—keep your money for some other that is to be sold!

LAFOUCHE. One hundred bid—it's a good price. He's yours, Mr. George Peyton. *(To Dido.)* Okay. What's your name, little wench?

DIDO. Dido.

LAFOUCHE. We'll start with Dido.

MINNIE. Wait! Actually…

> *Minnie goes over and whispers something in Lafouche's ear.*

LAFOUCHE. *(To George, incredulous.)* The property is requesting that it be sold along with another piece of property? *(Off George's shrug, with a sigh.)* You know what? This is a shitshow. Let's just get this over with. *(Back out.)* So, Dido here will be sold along with…?

MINNIE. Minerva. Minnie.

LAFOUCHE. With Minerva.

> *Minnie and Dido mount table and sort of stare at Ratts a lot, who seems to respond? Over the following, they somehow manage to seduce Ratts into buying them. It works.*

MINNIE. Haaaaaaaaaaaay.

LAFOUCHE. Shall we start the bidding at one thousand for the pair?

One thousand. Can I get fifteen hundred? Fifteen. Two thousand? Two thousand, to Captain Ratts. Can I get three thousand? Three thousand? Three thousand to you, Mr. M'Closky.

RATTS. Come on now! I really need some niggers! Please let me get what I came here for! Five thousand!

LAFOUCHE. Five thousand bid from Captain Ratts. Six? Six? Do I hear six? No. Five thousand bid from Captain Ratts. Going, going, gone. They're yours.

MINNIE. Yaaaaaaay!

Minnie and Dido dismount and go over to stand behind Ratts.

LAFOUCHE. What a steal. Next up is…a pregnant female field-hand…with other child. A fertile bargain. Three for the price of one.

Grace gets on the table holding her baby, which is, ideally, a white baby in blackface.

GRACE. *(To Ratts.)* Buy me, Mas'r Ratts, do buy me, sar.

RATTS. And what in thunder would I do with you and those devils on board my boat?

GRACE. Wash, sar—cook, sar—anything.

LAFOUCHE. Come now, captain. Don't separate this poor heifer from her little niglets.

RATTS. *(With a sigh.)* Fine. Eight hundred.

LAFOUCHE. Eight hundred. Do I heard nine? Nine. Nine hundred to Mr. M'Closky. One thousand. One thousand to Captain Ratts. Do I hear eleven? Eleven? Eleven? Eleven to M'Closky.

RATTS. I'm broke, dear—I'm sorry.

LAFOUCHE. All right: eleven hundred to M'Closky—going—going—sold!

Lafouche bangs his gavel.

MINNIE. *(Trying to start something.)* Who ghetto now, bitch?!

Commotion. Lafouche bangs his gavel.

LAFOUCHE. Settle down! Settle down! *(To George.)* I guess on to the property— *(Seeing Zoe hiding offstage.)* Actually, wait, no, I almost forgot: the octoroon girl, Zoe! Thank God.

Zoe enters, very pale, and stands on table—hitherto M'Closky has taken no real interest in the sale, now perks up.

GEORGE. *(Rising.)* Gentlemen, we are all acquainted with the circumstances of Miss Zoe's position, and I feel sure that no one here will oppose the family which desires to redeem the child of your esteemed and noble friend and my uncle, the late Judge Peyton.

RATTS. Here, here!

LAFOUCHE. While the proceeds of this sale obviously promises to realize far, far less than the debts upon it, it is my duty to prevent any collusion for the depreciation of the property. What is offered for Zoe?

GEORGE. One thousand dollars.

M'CLOSKY. Two thousand.

GEORGE. Three thousand.

M'CLOSKY. Five thousand.

GEORGE. Demon! Seven!

M'CLOSKY. Eight.

GEORGE. Nine.

M'CLOSKY. Ten. It's no use, squire.

RATTS. Jacob M'Closky, you shan't have that girl. Now, take care what you do. Twelve thousand.

M'CLOSKY. Shan't I! Fifteen thousand. Beat that any of ye.

LAFOUCHE. Fifteen thousand bid for the octoroon.

> *Enter Dora.*

DORA. Twenty thousand!

M'CLOSKY. Twenty-five thousand.

GEORGE. Yelping hound—take that.

> *George rushes M'Closky/himself, who draws his knife. They scuffle elaborately—the actor literally wrestling with himself. The crowd reacts accordingly—the melee going on for a long while, until George manages to disarm M'Closky and seems prepared to cut his throat.*

LAFOUCHE. Hold on—stand back.

> *Beat, as George/M'Closky disengage, exhausted.*

(*To George.*) This is your own house and we are under your uncle's roof, but recollect yourself. And ain't we forgetting there's a lady present?

The knives disappear.

If we can't behave like Christians, let's try and act like gentlemen. I believe none of us have two feelings about the conduct of this man; but he has the law on his side—We may regret it, but we must respect it. Mr. M'Closky has bid twenty-five thousand dollars for the octoroon. Is there any other bid? For the first time, twenty-five thousand—last time!

Brings gavel down.

To Jacob M'Closky, the octoroon girl, Zoe, twenty-five thousand dollars.

M'Closky jumps on up on his chair, throws money in the air, and makes it rain—perhaps literally, perhaps figuratively. The theatre is a space of infinite possibility. Tableau.

End of Act Three

ACT FOUR

The empty, unfortunate-looking theatre, again.

BJJ and Playwright step forward from the tableau and darkness falls. Eventually, they are joined by Assistant, who is busy dealing with the actors onstage, cleaning up, checking his email, etc.

BJJ. So I think I fucked up. I had this really amazing concept for how this would all work with my limited resources and then—

PLAYWRIGHT. I grossly underestimated the amount of white men I actually would need here—

BJJ. Especially in this act—Act Four—

PLAYWRIGHT. Which is actually the most important of all the acts in a melodrama.

BJJ. Act Four is the act which usually follows the Act Three "climax," which you just saw.

PLAYWRIGHT. The fourth act sort of makes or breaks a show.

BJJ. It's sort of the spine of the whole drama—

PLAYWRIGHT. The hinge around which everything turns—

BJJ. Not just in terms of the narrative but also just in terms of the sheer "theatre" of a piece. You have a lot of stuff to do and it's really hard.

PLAYWRIGHT. Not only do you have to get the A plot—

BJJ. In this case, the story of Zoe and the estate—

PLAYWRIGHT. To intersect with the B plot—

BJJ. In this case, the murder of Paul—

PLAYWRIGHT. But it's your last chance to really hit the audience with something big—

BJJ. Like your best "theatre trick," if you will.

PLAYWRIGHT. You have to push everything—actors, props, set, light—to the limit somehow.

BJJ. They used to call it the "Sensation Scene"—

PLAYWRIGHT. Because the idea is to overwhelm your audience's senses, to the end of building the truest illusion of reality—

BJJ. Regardless of whether or not it has anything to do with the plot.

PLAYWRIGHT. You're just supposed to make people think, for just a second, that what they're seeing is real and dangerous and sort of novel.

BJJ. Oh, and also, more often than not, Act Four is where the like moral of the play lives—

PLAYWRIGHT. Which is why I needed more white guys—

BJJ. Because we're going to talk about universal themes—

PLAYWRIGHT. *(Brandishing the gavel.)* Like justice!

BJJ. And not "social issues."

PLAYWRIGHT. You basically sort of give your audience the moral, then you overwhelm them with fake destruction.

BJJ. Or something. It's just so hard. So I'm just going to tell you what happens, so we can keep going. I hope that's okay.

PLAYWRIGHT. Basically, it's later that night, and we're at the wharf, where we find Captain Ratts and his people like loading up the ship.

BJJ. A bunch of other white guys are there—

PLAYWRIGHT. Including George and Pete, who've just dropped off their last load of cotton ever, I guess, and then M'Closky enters and he's like, for no reason, except for exposition and to be an asshole:

M'CLOSKY. You've got too much cotton onboard—it can barely stay above the water level—and there's a small freight of turpentine in the forehold there, and one of the barrels leaks; a spark from your engines might set the ship on fire, and you'll go with it.

PLAYWRIGHT. Then suddenly there's all this commotion!

BJJ. And everyone's all,

PLAYWRIGHT. "What's going on?"

BJJ. And somebody's like,

PLAYWRIGHT. "We found the Injun! We found Wahnotee, the murderer! Let's lynch him for killing that little nigger boy who used to sing for us!"

BJJ. And Wahnotee lumbers on, being chased by a bunch of people, and everyone's about to like jump on him and fuck him up—

PLAYWRIGHT. But George is all:

GEORGE. Hold on! No violence—the critter don't know what we mean!

PLAYWRIGHT. But M'Closky, the real murderer, is all,

M'CLOSKY. Let him answer for the boy then. Down with him—lynch him! And the crowd's like,

> *No one says anything for a second. BJJ and Playwright look at Assistant expectantly.*

ASSISTANT. "Lynch him!"

PLAYWRIGHT. And George's like:

GEORGE. Stan' back, I say! I'll nip the first that lays a finger on him—

BJJ. And they're basically all like,

PLAYWRIGHT. "But he killed the little slave boy who used to sing and dance for us!" And George's like,

GEORGE. I just don't think he killed Paul! It doesn't make any sense!

BJJ. And then someone's like,

PLAYWRIGHT. "Well we think he did kill him, so let's give him a trial like right now, since we've all got like fifteen minutes before we have to go—"

BJJ. And someone's like,

ASSISTANT. "Who will be the accuser?"

BJJ. And everyone's like,

ASSISTANT. "M'Closky!"

M'CLOSKY. Wait, why me?

ASSISTANT. And they're like,

PLAYWRIGHT. "Because you were the one who was just shouting to lynch him—"

M'CLOSKY. Fine. I know then that the boy was killed with that tomahawk—the redskin owns it—the signs of violence are all round the shed—ain't it clear that in a drunken fit he slew the boy and concealed the body yonder?

PLAYWRIGHT. And the crowd's all,

ASSISTANT. "Yeah! Yeah!" And then someone is like,

PLAYWRIGHT. "Who will defend the Indian?!"

ASSISTANT. And George's like,

GEORGE. I will, for it is against my nature to believe him guilty, and if he be, this isn't the place, nor you the authority, to try him. I appeal against your usurped authority; this lynch-law is a wild and lawless proceeding. You call yourselves judges—You aren't—You're a jury of executioners! Yonder, a poor, ignorant savage, and round him a circle of hearts, white with hate, thirsting for his blood: It is such scenes as these that bring disgrace upon our Western life.

M'CLOSKY. Evidence! Give us evidence! We've had talk enough; now for proof.

GEORGE. The proof is here, in my heart.

PETE. Stop, sar! Oh, laws-a-mussey—

BJJ. Oh right, also, like, randomly someone has brought on the camera that Wahnotee smashed after he found Paul dead—

PLAYWRIGHT. The same camera M'Closky stood in front of reading that letter—

BJJ. —And randomly, I guess, George never looked in the camera or forgot about the camera? This is actually a hole in Boucicault's plot. Not mine.

PLAYWRIGHT. Anyway, Pete's like:

PETE. See dis! Here's a pictur' I found stickin' in that yar telescope machine, sar! Look, sar!

GEORGE. A photographic plate. What's this, eh? Two forms! The child—'tis he! Dead—and above him—Ah! Ah! Jacob M'Closky, 'twas you murdered that—

Breaking character, becoming BJJ.

BJJ. Wait, hold on, can we actually…

Assistant nods and exits.

PLAYWRIGHT. You know, it's really hard to describe how this scene works—

BJJ. Because it actually would have been really exciting 150 years ago—having someone caught by a photograph.

PLAYWRIGHT. They were a very novel thing—

BJJ. Which is why this whole plot is more or less centered around a camera. But photographs to us? Boring. It's a cliché, but we've gotten so used to photos and photographic images that we've basically learned how to fake them, so the kind of justice around which this whole things hangs is actually a little dated—

PLAYWRIGHT. But part of the thrill, part of the "sensation" of the scene, was giving people back then a sense of having really witnessed something new and novel.

BJJ. And that's basically impossible for us to do now. If anything, the theatre is no longer a place of novelty. The fact is we can more or less experience anything nowadays. So I think the final frontier, awkwardly enough, is probably just an actual experience of finality, I think.

PLAYWRIGHT. Like—death, basically?

BJJ. So for a while I was thinking maybe I could actually just set this place on fire with you inside—

PLAYWRIGHT. Bring you as close to death as possible... That would be amazing...

BJJ. And then, of course, rescue each of you one by one—

PLAYWRIGHT. And then perform the rest of the show out on the street.

BJJ. But that would be crazy.

PLAYWRIGHT. And also I would only be able to do this show once.

BJJ. I thought about actually just sacrificing an animal onstage—

PLAYWRIGHT. Like in the good old days—A goat or something—

BJJ. But, there are laws against that, and, like, goats have nothing to do with—

PLAYWRIGHT. And you don't have a petting zoo—

BJJ. Anyway, I figured I'd try something. I hope it isn't too disappointing.

> *Assistant has wheeled out an overhead projector. He projects a lynching photograph onto the back wall.*

Where was—okay, sorry, I lost my place. I'm going to go back:

> *They perform the following in the light of the projection.*

GEORGE. I will, for it is against my nature to believe him guilty; and if he be, this isn't the place, nor you the authority, to try him. I appeal against your usurped authority; this lynch-law is a wild and lawless proceeding. You call yourselves judges—you aren't—you're a jury of executioners. Yonder, a poor, ignorant savage, and round him a circle of hearts, white with hate, thirsting for his blood. It is such scenes as these that bring disgrace upon our Western life.

M'CLOSKY. Evidence! Give us evidence. We've had talk enough; now for proof.

GEORGE. The proof is here, in my heart.

PETE. Stop, sar! Oh, laws-a-mussey, see dis! Here's a pictur' I found stickin' in that yar telescope machine, sar! Look, sar!

BJJ. I can't see anything. I'm sorry—Can we turn this off?

The picture disappears.

GEORGE. A photographic plate. What's this, eh? Two forms! The child—'tis he! Dead—and above him—Ah! Ah! Jacob M'Closky, 'twas you murdered that boy!

M'CLOSKY. Me?

GEORGE. You! You slew him with that tomahawk; and as you stood over his body with the letter in your hand, you thought that no witness saw the deed, that no eye was on you—but there was, Jacob M'Closky, there was. The eye of the Eternal was on you—the blessed sun in heaven, that, looking down, struck upon this plate the image of the deed.

M'CLOSKY. 'Tis false!

GEORGE. 'Tis true! The apparatus can't lie. Look there, jurymen. Oh, you wanted evidence—you called for proof—Heaven has answered and convicted you. You wanted to make us murder that Injinn; but since we've got our hands in for justice, we'll try it on you. Shall we have one law for the redskin and another for the white? Jacob, your accuser is that picture of the crime—let that speak—defend yourself.

PLAYWRIGHT. And M'Closky pulls out a knife.

M'CLOSKY. I will, quicker than lightning!

PLAYWRIGHT. And someone is like, "Seize him!" And all these men rush on M'Closky and take away his knife and then George is like,

GEORGE. Stop! Search him—we may find more evidence.

ASSISTANT. "Here's a letter!"

61

GEORGE. *(Opening the letter.)* What's here? "To Mrs. Peyton." Hello! I've got a hold of the tail of a rat. *(Reads.)* What's this? A draft for 85,000 dollars, and credit for the balance? You killed the boy to steal this letter from the mailbags—that the money should not arrive in time; had it done so, the lien on the estate would have ceased, and Zoe be free.

ASSISTANT. And everyone's like,

> *Everyone includes everyone on and offstage.*

EVERYONE. *(A loud, harsh, clear whisper.)* Lynch him!

GEORGE. Silence in the court: Stand back, let the gentlemen of the jury consult and return their verdict.

PETE. *(Showing Wahnotee the photo.)* See, Injun; look dar—You'se innocent—dar's de murderer of poor Paul.

WAHNOTEE. Ugh!

PETE. *Closky tue Paul*—kill de child with your tomahawk dar: 'twasn't you, no—Poor Injun lub our little Paul.

> *Wahnotee rises and looks at M'Closky.*

GEORGE. What say ye, gentlemen? Is the prisoner guilty, or is he not guilty?

ASSISTANT. And everyone's like,

EVERYONE. *(A loud, harsh, clear whisper.)* Guilty! Lynch him!

GEORGE. And what is to be his punishment?

EVERYONE. *(A loud, harsh, clear whisper.)* Death! Lynch him!

WAHNOTEE. *(Crossing to M'Closky.)* Ugh!

PETE. You're a dead man, Mas'r Closky—you got to b'lieve dat.

M'CLOSKY. No—no! You are a white man; you'll not leave one of your own blood to be butchered by the redskin? If I must die for what I have done, give me up to the law; but save me from the tomahawk. Let me be tried!

GEORGE. You have been tried—and convicted. Providence has chosen your executioner. I shan't interfere.

PETE. Oh, no; Mas'r George, don't leave Mas'r Closky like dat— 'tain't what a good Christian should do.

GEORGE. D'ye hear that, Jacob? This old nigger—the grandfather of the boy you murdered—speaks for you—don't that go through you?

WAHNOTEE. *(His hand on M'Closky's skull.)* WAHNOTEE!

GEORGE. *(Stopping Wahnotee.)* Whoa! No, Injun, we deal justice here, not revenge; t'isn't you he has injured, 'tis the white man, whose laws he has offended.

PLAYWRIGHT. So Captain Ratts tells Pete and some men to put M'Closky into the hold or hatch to await, I guess, his hanging or whatever, and they take him down into the hatch or the hold or whatever it's called and everyone's like, "Well that's over," and go back to business as usual.

> *Beat.*

But then, like thirty seconds later, Pete comes running up being like—!

> *Assistant/Pete comes running back in.*

PETE. O, lawd, dat debil Closky, he tore hisself from de gent'lam, knock me down, take my light, and trows it on de turpentine barrels, and now de cabin's all afire!

> *Fire sounds. The sounds of men panicking. Actual fire would be great. Pete exits.*

PLAYWRIGHT. And basically the entire boat is on fire! And you sort of see the flames engulfing everything—all the cotton—everything!

ASSISTANT. There's general chaos—men running around, panicking, exiting the boat—an alarm starts ringing—and then M'Closky:

M'CLOSKY. Ha! Burn! Burn! That's right. You thought you had cornered me, did ye? And now the road to escape is clear before me—and thus to secure it!

WAHNOTEE. *(Appearing, raising his tomahawk.)* Paul.

M'CLOSKY. Devil!—you still here?!

> *Pulls out his knife.*

—Stand clear!

> *Wahnotee strikes the knife out of his hand with his tomahawk and then M'Closky starts to back away but Wahnotee throws off his blanket and strikes at M'Closky several times, who avoids him, before he catches his arm, and they struggle violently for the tomahawk, but Wahnotee wins, obviously, and drags him along the ground, taking up M'Closky's knife and repeatedly*

> *stabs him with it, until M'Closky is bloody and nearly dead but still screaming. It seems incredibly real. And then Wahnotee finds some rope and wraps it around M'Closky's neck, starts dragging him off.*

SOMEBODY! *(Choking.)* HELP! HELP! HELP! HELP! HELP! HELP! HELP! HELP! HELP! HELP! HELP! HELP! HELP! HELP! HELP! HELP!

> *They exit as the noise and the flames build and build and build and build before, suddenly, lights and sound cut out completely, everything plunged in darkness and quiet. Assistant wanders in, lit only by a small flame or lantern, which he carries.*

ASSISTANT. *(In darkness.)* Then the boat explodes.

> *His light goes out. Perhaps, in the darkness, cotton rains down on the audience.*

Sensation.

> *Beat.*

Anyway. The point of this whole thing was to make you feel something.

> *Assistant exits.*

End of Act Four

ACT FIVE

Outside the sole lit cabin in the abandoned negroes quarters. It is night. Zoe is discovered.

ZOE. It wants some hours yet to daylight and soon that man—M'Closky—my master, will come for me. He has paid my price, and he only consented to let me remain here this one night, because Mrs. Peyton promised to give me up to him today. Where is the negroes quarters? Ah, yes. Here they are—

Knocks.

They are abandoned but—no; I see a light.

DIDO. *(Entering from cabin.)* Who dat?

ZOE. Mammy! 'Tis I—Zoe.

DIDO. *(Taken aback by her word choice, then:)* Missey Zoe! Why are you out in de swamp dis time ob night? And you is all wet! Missey Zoe, you catch de fever for sure!

ZOE. Aunty, that is why I've come. There is already sickness up at the house: I have been up all night beside one who suffers, and, Mammy, you are wise—you know every plant, don't you, and what it is good for? I remembered that when I had the fever you gave me a drink, a bitter drink that made me sleep—do you remember it?

DIDO. Dat drink is fust rate for de fever. Is de folks head bad?

ZOE. Very bad, Mammy; and the heart aches worse, so they can get no rest.

DIDO. Hold on a bit, I get you a bottle.

Dido exits into the cabin. Zoe is alone for a bit. An owl hoots. Dido reenters with a bottle.

Here 'tis—now you give one timbleful—dat's nuff.

ZOE. All there is there would kill one, wouldn't it?

DIDO. Guess it could kill a dozen.

ZOE. It's not a painful death, Mammy, is it? You told me it produced a long, long sleep.

DIDO. Why you speak so wild? What you's gwine to do, missey? Why you tremble so?

ZOE. Give it to me.

DIDO. No. You want to hurt yourself! O, Zoe, why you ask Dido for dis pizin?

ZOE. Listen to me. I love one who is here, and he loves me—George. I sat outside his door all night and heard his sighs—his agony—torn from him by my coming fate; and he said, "I'd rather see her dead than his!"

DIDO. Dead!

ZOE. He said so before he left for the landing with Pete. I cried for hours before I rose up with the resolve to end my own life! For his sake! I stole from the house, and ran down to the bayou; but its cold, black stream terrified me—drowning must be so horrible a death. I could not do it. Then, as I knelt there, weeping for courage, a snake rattled beside me. I shrunk from it and fled. Death was right there next me, and I dared not take it. O! I'm afraid to die; yet I am more afraid to live.

DIDO. Die!

ZOE. So I came here to you; to you, my own dear mammy, who so often hushed me to sleep when I was a child. You can protect me from the man—do let me die without pain, that I may never leave my home—my dear, dear home.

DIDO. No, no—

ZOE. O! Good, good nurse: you will not give me to that man? Your own Zoe, that loves you, Mammy, so much—

> *Gets bottle away from Dido.*

Ah! I have it.

DIDO. No, missey. O! no—don't!

ZOE. Hush!

> *Zoe runs off. Dido looks off after her, sort of upset. Minnie comes to the door, holding a jug of something. She's a little tipsy.*

MINNIE. Girl, who was that?

DIDO. Zoe. That bitch just ran off wit all your medicine—I think she about to poison herself!

66

MINNIE. What? Why?

DIDO. Cuz she in love wit that white man.

MINNIE. *(Shaking her head.)* Hmhmhm. Zoe is such a mess.

> *They both look off after Zoe for a beat. Dido is clearly upset about something. It takes a moment to surface.*

DIDO. And you know she kept calling me "Mammy"! And I was like, bitch, what? We are basically the same age!

MINNIE. Whaaaat?

DIDO. I can't believe that shit. Do I look that old to you?

MINNIE. No, girl. Black don't crack. That bitch is just crazy. That's what happens when you hang out wit all these damn white people all the damn time. Let it go.

DIDO. Naw, Minnie! Shit!

MINNIE. Come on, girl! Stop freaking out. She ain't worth it. We 'bout to be livin' on a boat and here you are letting these lightskinned haters get you down. Come on, help me finish packing.

> *Beat.*

DIDO. *(Collecting herself.)* You right. Moving just always be stressin' me out.

MINNIE. I know, right?

DIDO. Heifer, how would you know? You been on this plantation yo' whole life!

MINNIE. Oh, right.

> *Beat.*

DIDO. *(Sucks her teeth.)* And how are you just now starting to pack when we leaving in like an hour?

MINNIE. I ain't know it took this long. I ain't neva had to move before, girl.

DIDO. It's wrapping up all yo' damn Voodoo dolls that's taking so damn long.

MINNIE. *(Hurt.)* Girl, those are my collectibles…

> *Beat.*

Why are you freakin' out at me like this? I thought we wuz girls?

Beat.

DIDO. *(Collecting herself.)* I'm sorry, Minnie. I just don't like when people be treating me like I'm some old woman. I am not a mammy! I'm not!

MINNIE. *(Realizes why Dido is upset, then.)* It's okay, girl. I forgive you.

> *Embraces her.*

But we gotta be good to one anutha. You know all we got is each other now.

DIDO. You right.

> *They un-embrace.*

You think we should go tell somebody?

MINNIE. Tell somebody what?

DIDO. That Zoe is 'bout to poison herself.

MINNIE. Who you gonna tell?

DIDO. I don't know. Mrs. Peyton?

MINNIE. Girl, stop. These people ain't our problem anymore. We 'bout to be livin' on a boat!

> *Looks at Dido, who seems unexcited.*

I'm worried about you.

DIDO. Why?

MINNIE. I think you can get too worked up over small stuff. Stop being so sensitive and caring so much about other people and what they think about you or you gonna catch yourself a stroke, for real. You can't be bringing your work home with you. If Zoe's lightskinned ass wanna call you old and go poison herself over some white man, then you need to let her do that and move on. She's an adult. You can't change her. Shit. Same thing with Mrs. Peyton. And Miss Dora. And Mas'r George. And Mas'r M'Closky. I know we slaves and evurthang, but you are not your job. You gotta take time out of your day to live life for you.

> *Dido starts crying, softly.*

Oh, girl! What's wrong?

DIDO. I just don't know what I'm supposed to be doing better.

MINNIE. What?

DIDO. To be happy. I don't like feeling the way I do. This life—I didn't ask for it.

MINNIE. Didn't nobody ask for they lives, girl.

DIDO. I know. I just don't know what I'm supposed to do with that.

Minnie comforts her.

MINNIE. Well, listen: I'll tell you what you need to do right now. You need to come back inside, help me finish packing, have one more drink, get a little catnap, put on your nice slave tunic, and get ready for your life to change. We 'bout to be on a boat, and it may not be heaven, but it's sho' as hell different than this here swamp and that's got to mean something. Plus, I'm getting cold standing out here.

DIDO. Yeah, let's go back inside.

They start to head back in.

MINNIE. You know, I would be so pissed if something were to happen that somehow rendered these last twelve hours totally moot.

DIDO. I know right? I was thinking the same thing. Like if these white folks found out like…Mas'r Closky like…killed Paul or something to intercept the letter that was supposed to save the plantation.

MINNIE. Wait—there was a letter that was supposed to save the plantation?

DIDO. Yes, girl. Haven't you heard Zoe and Mrs. Peyton going on and on about it? Every breakfast they been talking about it.

MINNIE. They do?

DIDO. Yes, girl. Where is your mind?

MINNIE. I must have zoned out. You know I be getting so bored.

DIDO. Girl, you are such a trip. Anyway, finish telling me about that rabbit.

Minnie and Dido exit, and the little light there is slowly starts to fade. Meanwhile, there are night sounds: crickets chirping, an owl's hoot. And, right before it gets too dark to see, Br'er Rabbit wanders in with a gavel and a tomahawk. As the lights fully die, he looks right as us. Then a blackout, in which there is singing. Everyone sings.

End of Play

PROPERTY LIST
(Use this space to create props lists for your production)

SOUND EFFECTS

(Use this space to create sound effects lists for your production)

Note on Songs/Recordings, Images, or Other Production Design Elements

Be advised that Broadway Licensing neither holds the rights to nor grants permission to use any songs, recordings, images, or other design elements mentioned in the play. It is the responsibility of the producing theater/organization to obtain permission of the copyright owner(s) for any such use. Additional royalty fees may apply for the right to use copyrighted materials.

For any songs/recordings, images, or other design elements mentioned in the play, works in the public domain may be substituted. It is the producing theater/organization's responsibility to ensure the substituted work is indeed in the public domain. Broadway Licensing cannot advise as to whether or not a song/arrangement/recording, image, or other design element is in the public domain.